learn to draw

Exotic Animals

Step-by-step instructions for more than 25 unusual animals

ILLUSTRATED BY ROBBIN CUDDY

Quarto Library

This library edition published in 2016 by Walter Foster Jr.,
an imprint of Quarto Publishing Group USA Inc.
6 Orchard Road, Suite 100
Lake Forest, CA 92630

Distributed in the United States and Canada by
Lerner Publisher Services
241 First Avenue North
Minneapolis, MN 55401 U.S.A.
www.lernerbooks.com

First Library Edition

Library of Congress Cataloging-in-Publication Data

Learn to draw exotic animals : step-by-step instructions for more than 25 exotic animals / illustrated by Robbin Cuddy. -- First Library Edition.
pages cm
ISBN 978-1-939581-97-6
1. Animals in art--Juvenile literature. 2. Exotic animals--Juvenile literature. 3. Drawing--Technique-- Juvenile literature. I. Cuddy, Robbin, illustrator.
NC780.L335 2015
743.6--dc23

2015031439

9 8 7 6 5 4 3 2 1

MIX
Paper from responsible sources
FSC® C008080

Table of Contents

Tools & Materials

There's more than one way to bring exotic animals to life on paper—you can use crayons, markers, colored pencils, or even paints. Just be sure you have plenty of good animal colors—grays, browns, blacks, oranges, and reds.

How to Use This Book

The drawings in this book are made up of basic shapes, such as circles, triangles, and rectangles. Practice drawing the shapes below.

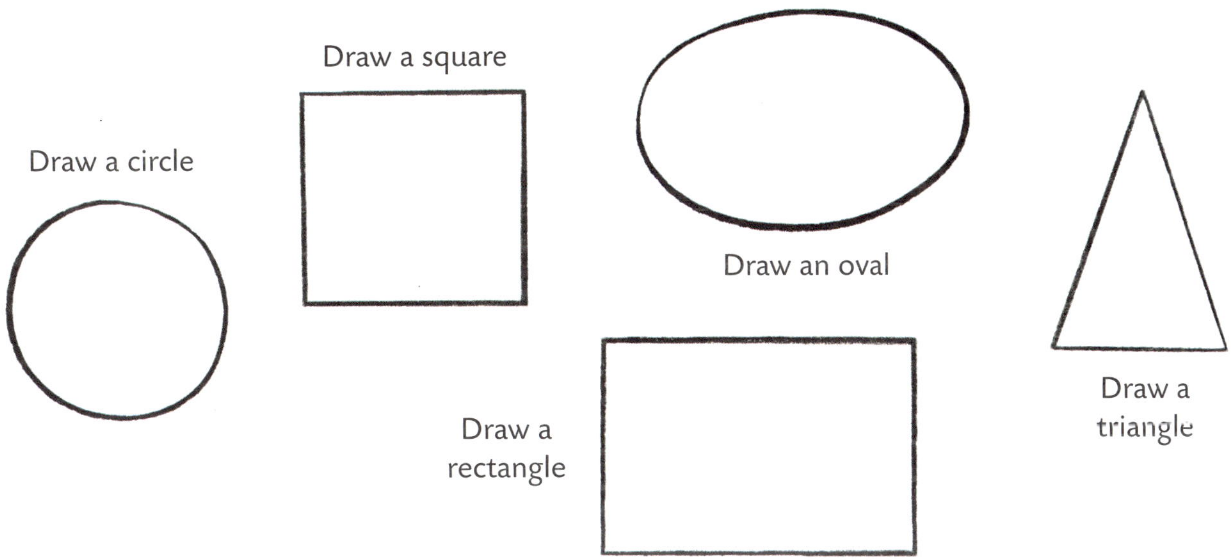

Notice how these drawings begin with basic shapes.

In this book, you'll learn about the size, weight, diet, location, and appearance of each featured exotic animal. Look for mini quizzes along the way to learn new and interesting facts!

Look for this symbol, and check your answers on page 64!

Exotic Animals of the World

This book will take you on a journey across the world, from the African savannah to the rainforests of South America. Along the way, you'll encounter some of the most colorful and unique animals on earth. View the map below to see where you can find them.

Asia
Africa
Australia

Arabian Camel

Details

Size: 5.5 to 7 feet tall
Weight: 700 to 1,500 pounds
Diet: Desert vegetation
Location: Northern and Eastern Africa, the Middle East, and other parts of Southwest Asia

Did You Know?

There are over 160 words for "camel" in the Arabic language.

Also called the "dromedary," this one-humped pack animal has long eyelashes, closable nostrils, kneepads, and other unique adaptations for a hot and sandy life in the desert.

1

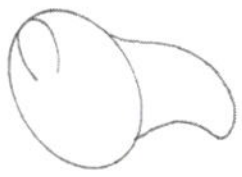

2

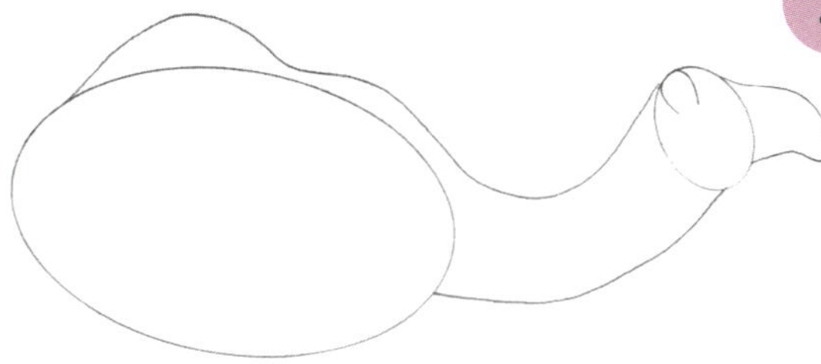

3

4

5

6

Fun Fact!

A thirsty camel can drink up to 30 gallons of water in just 13 minutes.

Boa Constrictor

Details

Size: 13 feet long
Weight: 100 pounds
Diet: Rats, lizards, birds, eggs, monkeys, and other small mammals
Location: Central and South America

Did You Know?

The boa constrictor uses sharp, curved teeth to grip its prey. Then the snake coils around and constricts (or squeezes) the animal. Once the prey has died or lost consciousness, the boa can swallow it without a fight. No chewing necessary!

This large snake is known for its thick, muscular body and wide, tooth-lined jaws, which can open up to swallow its prey whole!

1

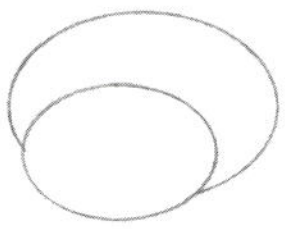

2

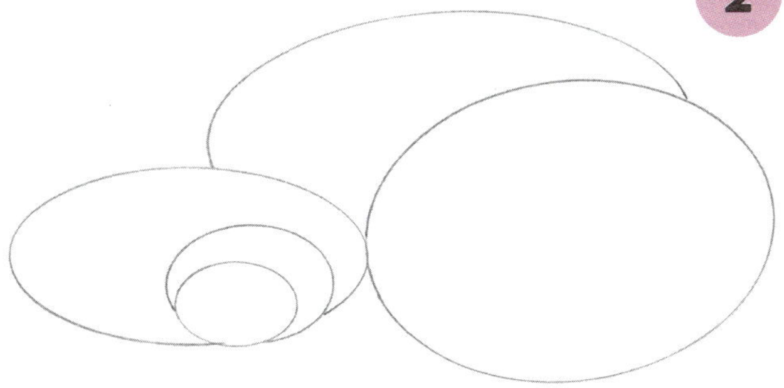

3

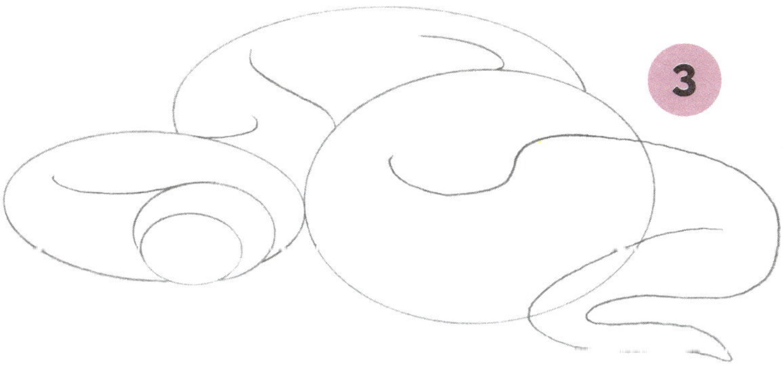

4

5

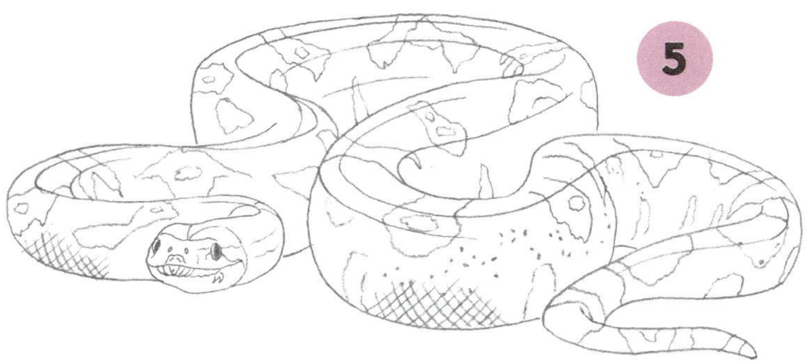

6

Mini Quiz

True or False: Boa constrictors come in a wide variety of colors and feature a range of markings.

(Answer on page 64)

Squirrel Monkey

Fun Fact!

The squirrel monkey has a tail that is longer than its body! The lengthy, bushy-tipped tail helps it keep balance as it moves through the canopies of the rainforest.

The squirrel monkey is a small tree-dwelling primate with a light eye mask, a black-skinned muzzle, and soft fur that ranges from white, gray, and black to bright orange.

Mini Quiz

True or False: Squirrel monkeys are *nocturnal*, which means that they are most active at night.

(Answer on page 64)

Woolly Monkey

Details

Size: 2 feet tall
Weight: 11 to 18 pounds
Diet: Fruit, flowers, leaves, nuts, and small animals
Location: South America

Mini Quiz

What is the proper term for a group of woolly monkeys?

A. Band
B. Troop
C. Clan
D. Pride

(Answer on page 64)

Covered in thick brown or gray fur, woolly monkeys are some of the largest primates of the New World. They have round heads, flat muzzles, and long, strong tails.

1

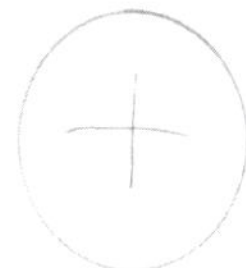

2

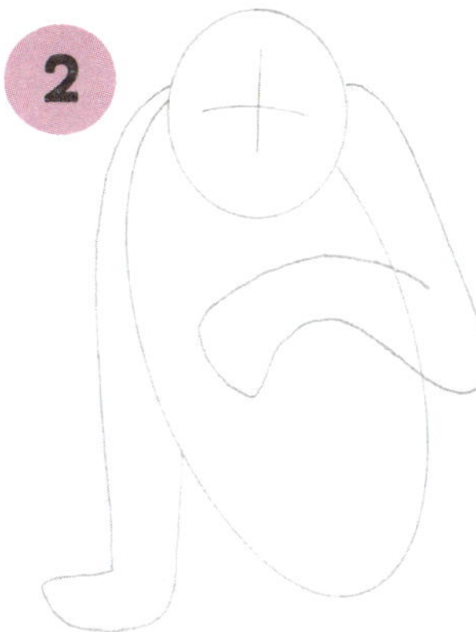

3

4

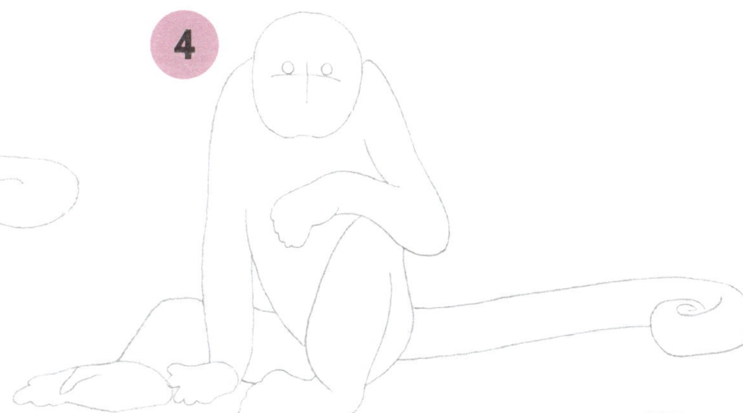

5

6

Fun Fact!

Like many New World monkeys, the woolly monkey has a *prehensile tail*. This kind of tail acts as a fifth limb that can grasp and help the monkey climb through trees.

Panther Chameleon

Did You Know?

Roughly half of Earth's chameleon species come from Madagascar—a large island off the southeastern coast of Africa that is known for its unique animals.

The panther chameleon is a reptile with skin that can change to vibrant colors. The chameleon has a striped back, coiled tail, and pinhole pupils.

1

2

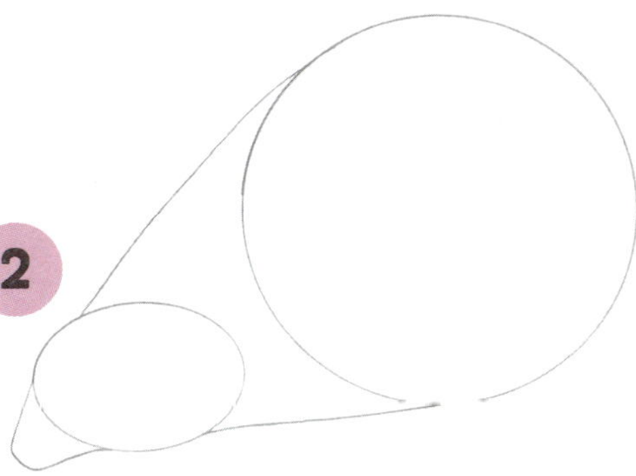

3

4

5

6

Fun Fact!

When relaxed, the panther chameleon is a greenish color, allowing it to blend into the trees. When excited, it changes its skin to red and orange. This transformation is due to nanocrystals in its layers of skin.

Eastern Coral Snake

Details

Size: 3 feet long
Diet: Frogs, lizards, and other snakes
Location: North, Central, and South America

Did You Know?

People often confuse this snake with the nonvenomous scarlet kingsnake, which bears red, black, and white bands. Here is a popular rhyme to help you tell the difference:

Red and yellow
can kill a fellow;
Red touches black,
friend of Jack.

This venomous snake has wide red and black bands separated by thinner bands of yellow. It lives in a variety of habitats, from dry shrub areas to forests and swamp edges.

1

2

3

4

5

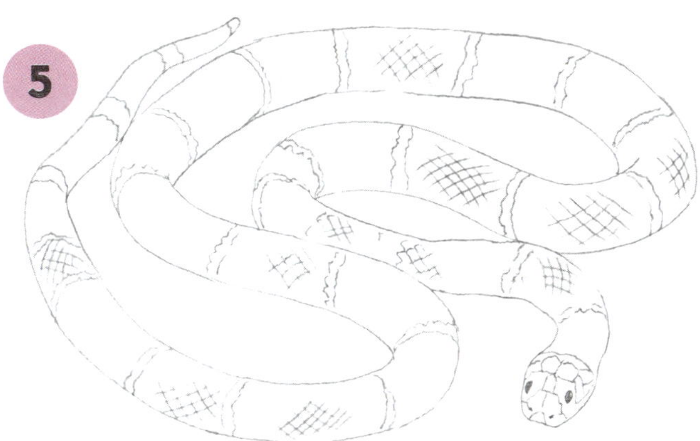

6

Mini Quiz

Which of the following are other names for the eastern coral snake?

A. Harlequin snake
B. American cobra
C. Florida coral snake
D. All of the above

(Answer on page 64)

Degu

Location: Chile, South America

Size: 10 to 12 inches

Weight: Less than 1 pound

Diet: Grasses, shrubs, seeds

Did You Know?

In addition to strong incisors (front teeth), rodents have cheek teeth. These are flat-topped, molar-like teeth that help rodents grind up vegetation. A degu's cheek tooth looks like a figure-8, which inspired its Latin name, *octodon degus.*

The degu is an intelligent rodent with large, rounded ears and brown fur. Native to the country of Chile, these social critters live in complex soft-soil burrows.

1

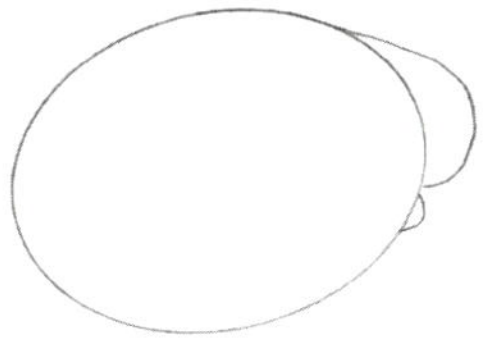

2

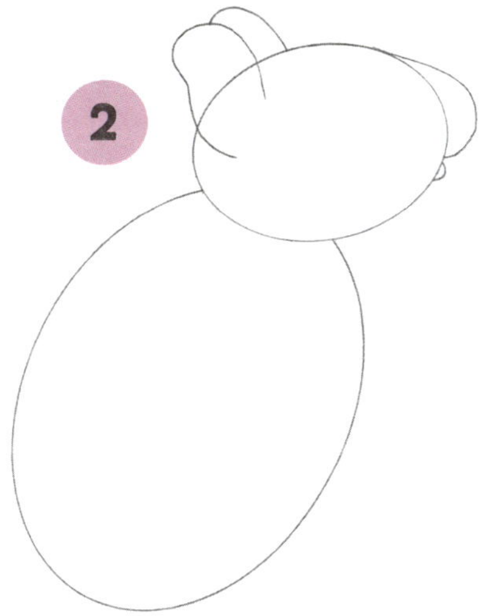

3

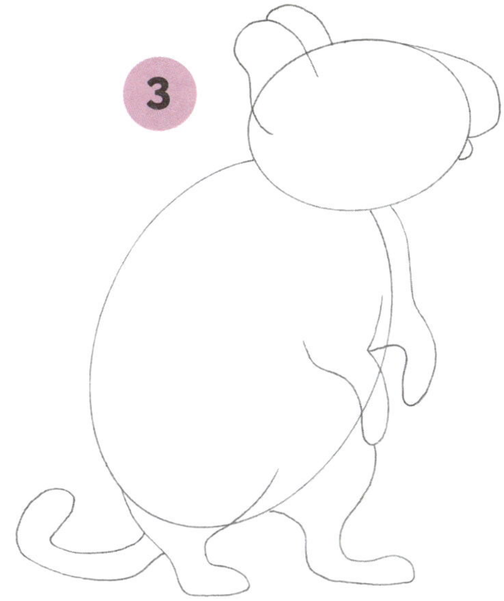

4

5

6

Fun Fact!

This relative of the guinea pig and chinchilla has recently become a popular pet. The degu is easy to care for, active, and clever.

Red Panda

Details

Size: 2 feet long
Weight: 15 pounds
Diet: Bamboo, leaves, flowers, and bird eggs
Location: Asia

Did You Know?

This tree-dwelling animal is about the size of a cat. Despite its name, the red panda is more like a raccoon than a bear. The word "panda" refers to the Nepalese word poonya, defined as "eater of bamboo."

These skilled climbers have rust-colored fur, distinct brown and white facial markings, and bushy, ringed tails. They make their home in the Himalayas.

1

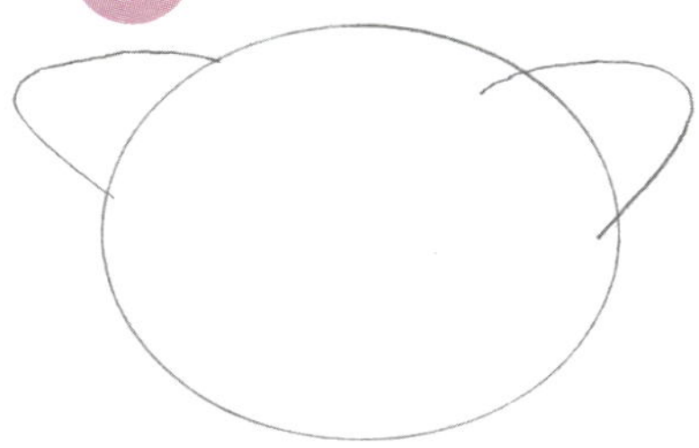

2

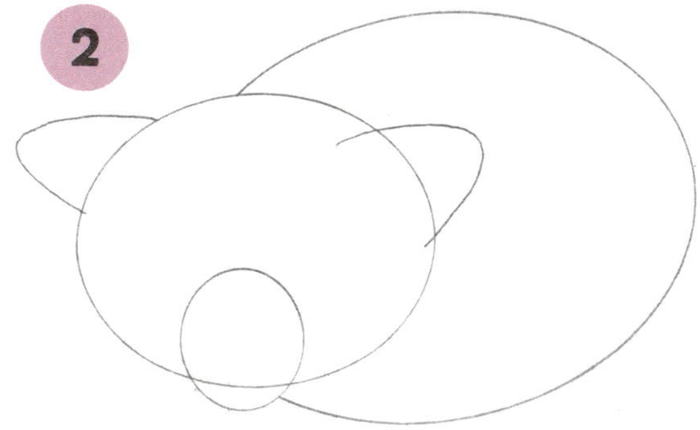

3

4

5

6

Fun Fact!

Although they have intimidating claws and sharp teeth, red pandas are generally considered friendly and are known for their ability to be tamed.

Gaur

Details

Size: 10 feet long
Weight: 1,500 to 3,000 pounds
Diet: Leaves, herbs, flowers, and fruit
Location: India and Southeast Asia

Did You Know?

The gaur is one of the largest land animals on earth! It has high shoulders and a muscular body, with a prominent ridge along its back. Bulls (male gaurs) are larger than cows (female gaurs).

This wild cattle has dark skin, white leg "stockings," wide ears, a square muzzle, and two thick horns that curve up and inward.

1

2

3

4

5

6

Mini Quiz

Gaurs typically have _____ eyes.

A. Blue

B. Green

C. Yellow

D. Brown

(Answer on page 64)

Mandarin Fish

Details

Size: 4 inches long
Diet: Worms, eggs, and small marine animals
Location: Pacific Ocean

Did You Know?

Only two species of vertebrates contain blue pigment in their cells—and the Mandarin fish is one of them! Other species that appear to have blue coloring, such as butterflies, birds, and beetles, do not have blue pigment; instead, they feature structures that reflect blue.

Covered in brilliant neon markings, the colorful Mandarin fish dwells in the coral reefs and shallow lagoons of the Pacific Ocean.

1

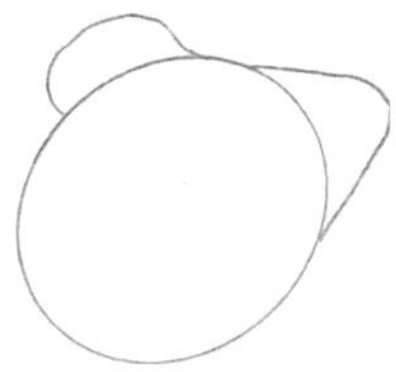

2

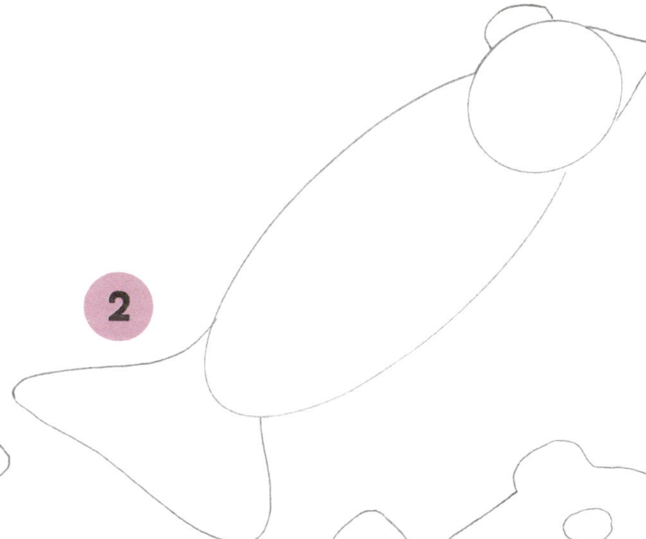

3

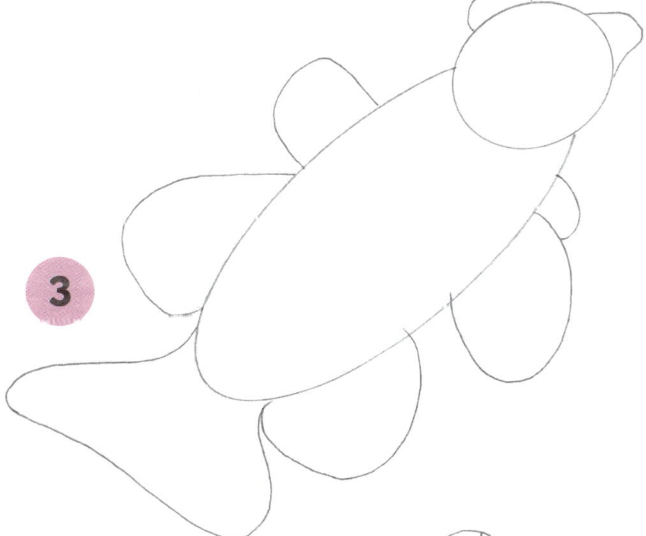

4

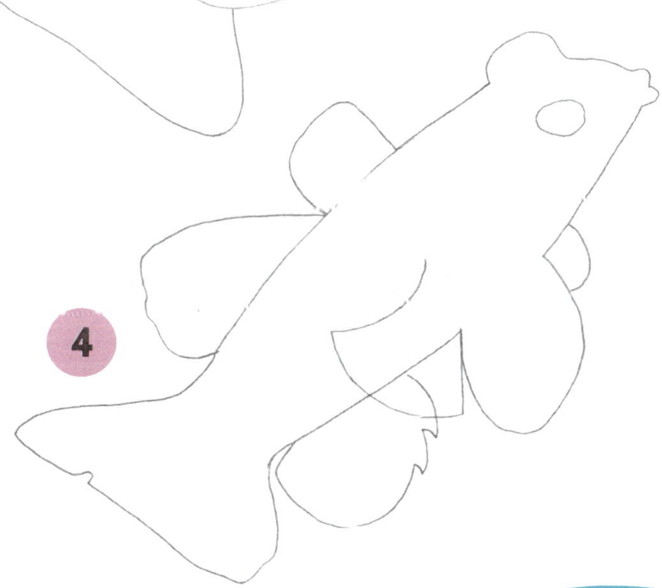

5

6

Fun Fact!

The Mandarin fish doesn't have teeth near its lips, but it has teeth in its throat! Called "pharyngeal teeth," these structures help the fish crush its food while swallowing.

Geoffroy's Cat

Did You Know?

Although most have black-spotted coats, some have an entirely black coat. These individuals are called "melanistic."

Known for its excellent climbing and swimming skills, this feline has a black-spotted coat and a white-tipped tail.

Fun Fact!

This feline was named after Étienne Geoffroy Saint-Hilaire (1772–1844)—a French naturalist and professor known for his animal classification.

1

2

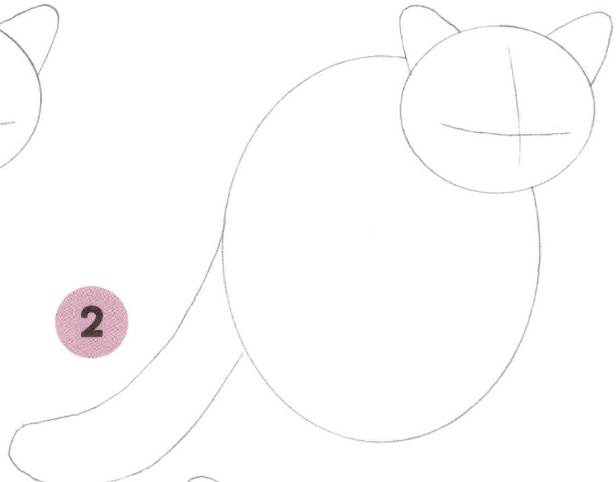

3

4

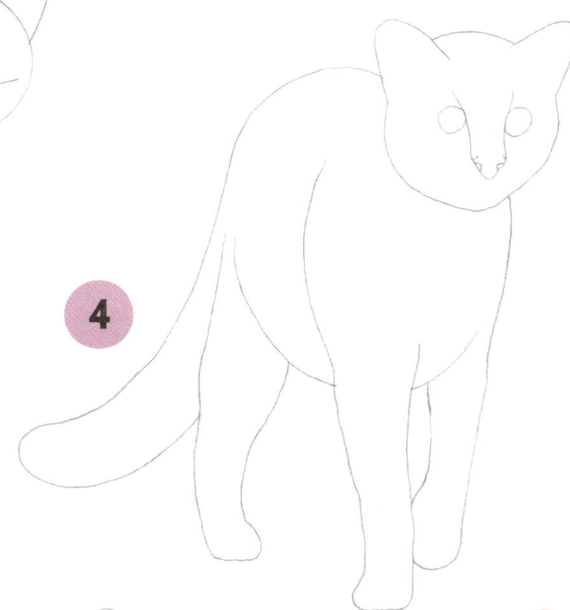

5

6

Hyacinth Macaw

Mini Quiz

Hyacinth macaws can generally live to be — years old.

A. 20
B. 30
C. 40
D. 50

(Answer on page 64)

The endangered hyacinth macaw has brilliant blue feathers, dark-tipped wings, yellow facial markings, and a sharply curved beak.

Fun Fact!

With a wingspan of 4 feet, the hyacinth macaw is the largest member of the parrot family. Like other parrots, this macaw is loud with a playful and affectionate personality.

1

2

3

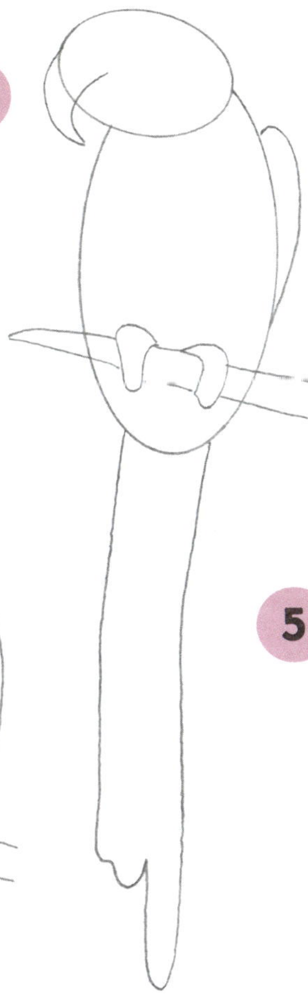

4

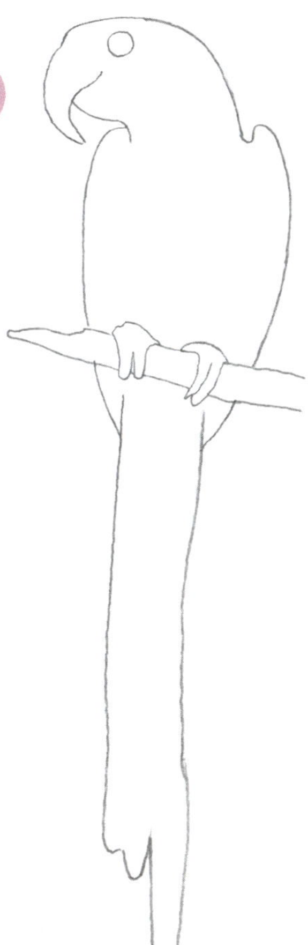

5

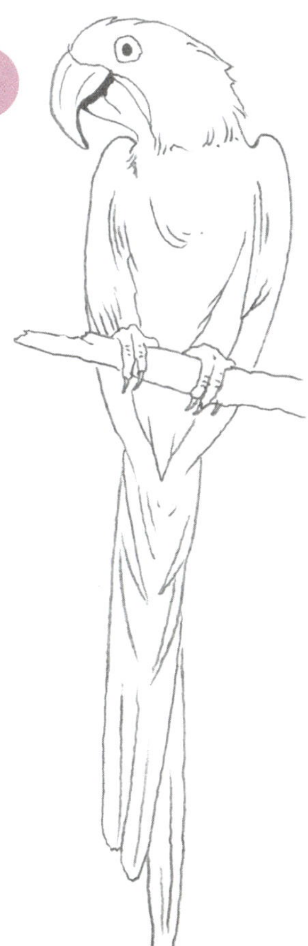

6

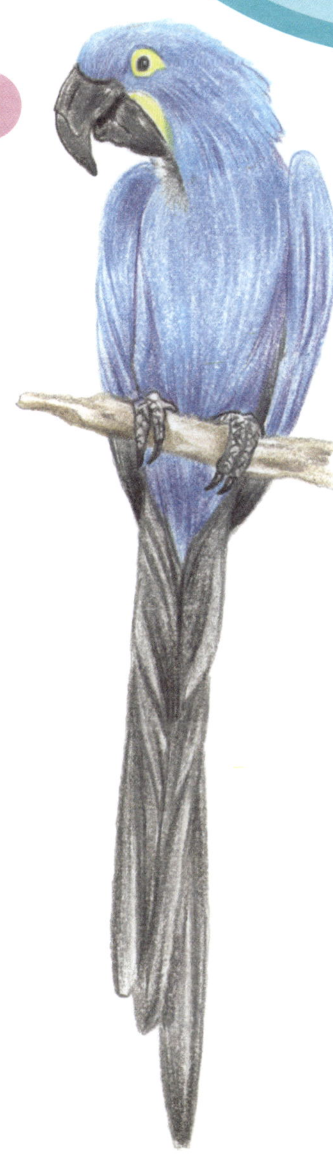

Rhinoceros Hornbill

Did You Know?

Resembling a second bill on the bird's face, the hornlike growth on the rhinoceros hornbill is called a "casque." Made of keratin, this hollow structure helps carry the calls and honks of the bird as it communicates with other hornbills.

The rhinoceros hornbill is a black-feathered bird with an orange hornlike feature above its beak. Its white tail has a black horizontal band.

1

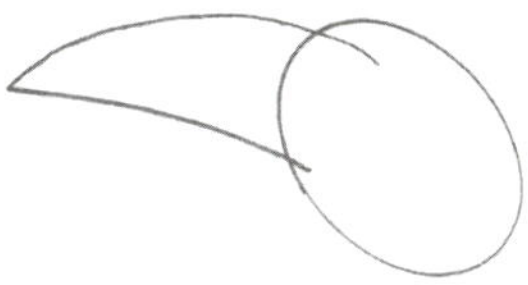

2

3

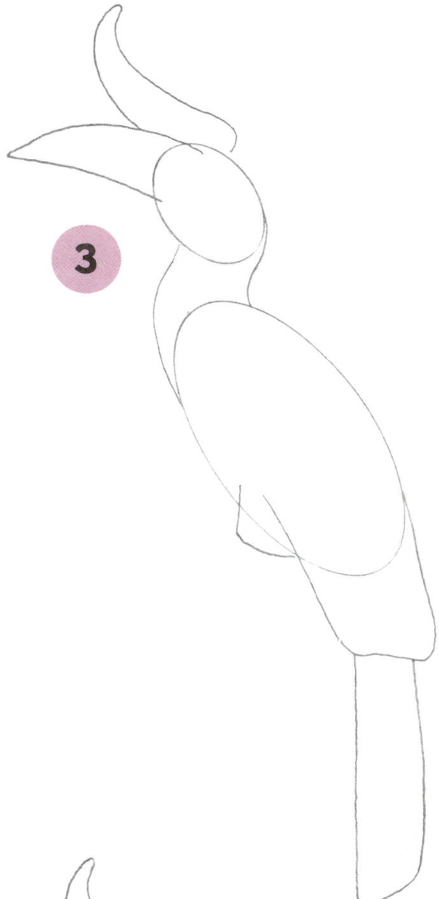

Fun Fact!

It's easy to tell the difference between a male and a female of this species. The female rhinoceros hornbill has white eyes, whereas the male has deep red eyes!

4

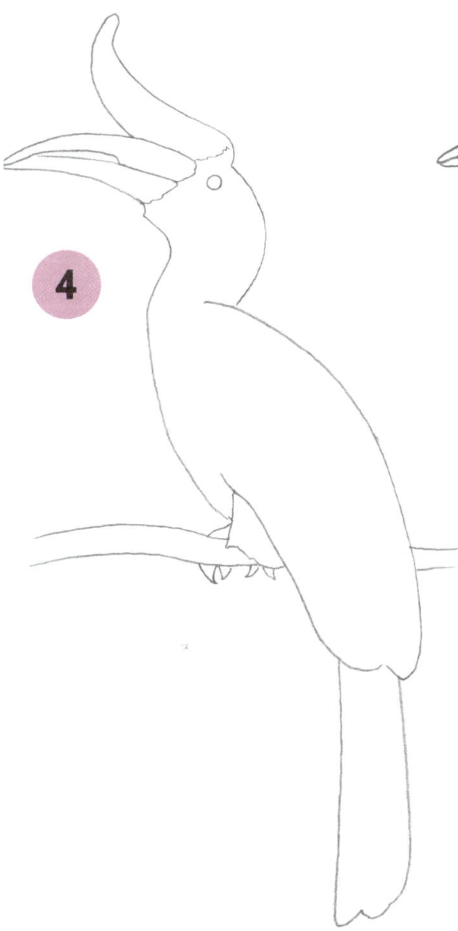

5

6

Ferret

Details

Size: About 20 inches long
Weight: 1 to 5 pounds
Diet: Rodents, rabbits, and birds
Location: Across the northern hemisphere

Did You Know?

There are two species of ferret: the common ferret and the black-footed ferret. Domesticated ferrets are common ferrets, but the wild, black-footed ferret is an endangered species.

The ferret has a slender body, a long neck, and short limbs. This cute critter also has a pointed nose, rounded ears, and whiskers.

1

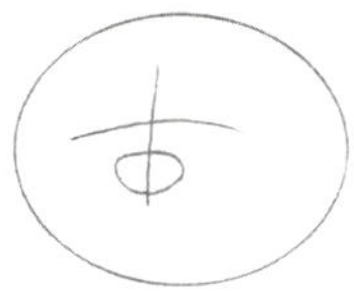

2

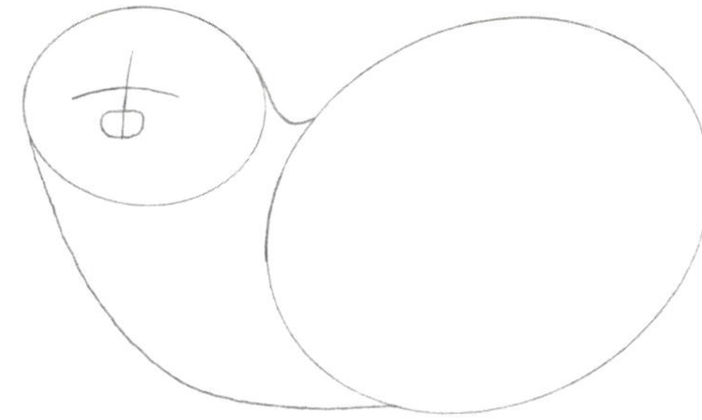

3

4

5

6

Fun Fact!

A group of ferrets is called a "business."

Pangolin

Details

Size: 2 feet long
Weight: 60 pounds
Diet: Termites, ants, and other insects
Location: Asia and Africa

Did You Know?

Pangolin scales are not like the scales of a fish or reptile. Instead, they are actually made of compressed hairs that feel like fingernails!

The pangolin is a tropical mammal with brown, overlapping scales. It has a cone-shaped head, a long tail, and a sticky, wormlike tongue.

1

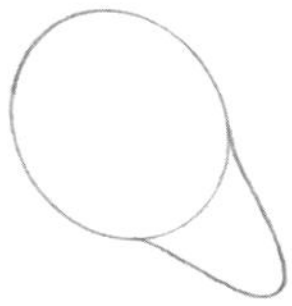

2

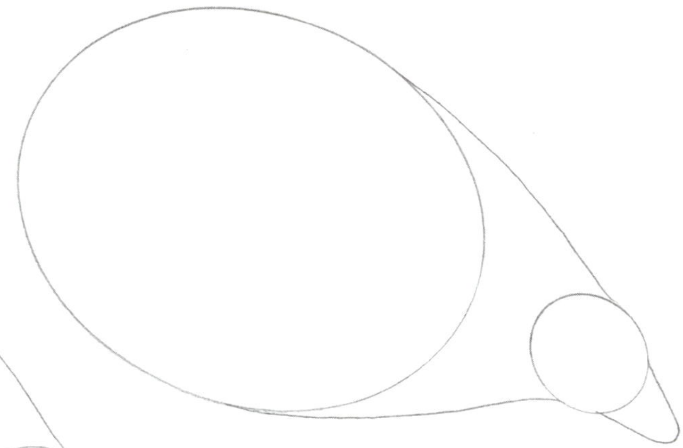

3

4

5

6

Fun Fact!

The sticky tongue of the pangolin is very long—even longer than the pangolin's entire body! It connects deep inside the body, near the pelvis.

Poison Dart Frog

Details

Size: 0.5 to 2.5 inches long
Weight: Less than 1 ounce
Diet: Insects, such as crickets, flies, ants, and beetles
Location: Central and South America

Did You Know?

The poison dart frog can be a number of different colors—from black and white to red, orange, yellow, blue, and green. Its bright colors and eye-catching designs warn predators that it is poisonous.

The poison dart frog is a small, colorful amphibian with poisonous skin secretions. It lives near water in the tropics of Central and South America.

Fun Fact!

Some tribes in South America tip their hunting darts with the frog's poison by rubbing the darts along its back. It is said that one small frog has enough poison to kill ten men!

1

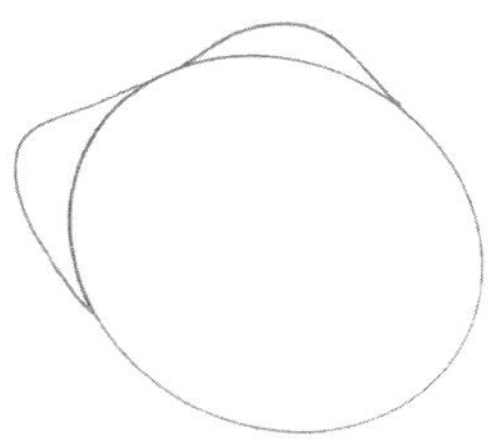

2

3

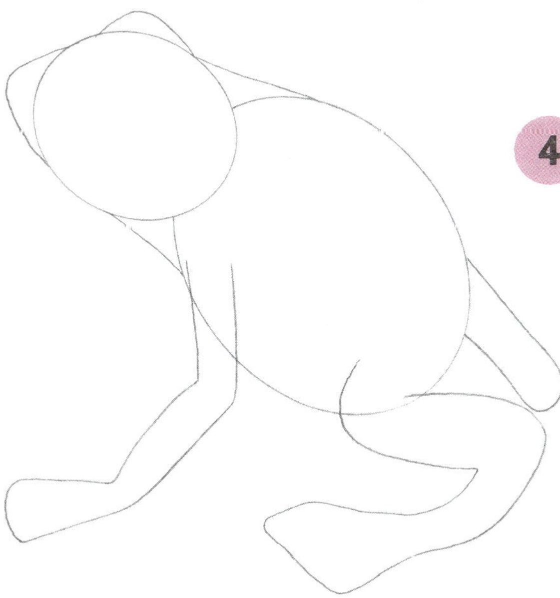

4

5

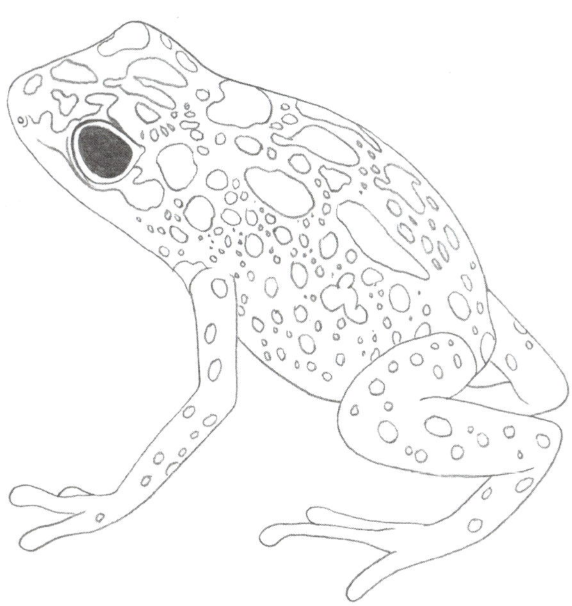

6

Vicuña

Did You Know?

The vicuña's coat is two-toned: reddish brown on the back, and white on the underside. The hair on it's chest is long, soft, and insulating, which keeps the vicuña warm during the cold winters of its high-elevation habitat.

The vicuña is a member of the camel family and has tall legs, a long neck, large ears, and a soft, fine coat. It lives in the grasslands of the Andes Mountains.

1

2

3

4

5

6

Mini Quiz

Which of the following is NOT a close relative of the vicuña?

A. Camel

B. Llama

C. Deer

D. Alpaca

(Answer on page 64)

Babirusa

Details

Size: 30 inches tall at the shoulder
Weight: 200 pounds
Diet: Fruit, leaves, grasses, mushrooms, insects, larvae, and small animals
Location: Indonesian islands

Did You Know?

These wrinkly beasts live in the forests of the Indonesian islands. They hunt and forage at night and sleep during the day. Surprisingly, babirusas are great swimmers and can be seen swimming in the ocean between islands!

The babirusa is a wild pig with gray skin, long legs, and a tapering snout. The male has four thin, curved tusks on its head.

Fun Fact!

The unusual tusks of the male babirusa are actually canine teeth. The top two teeth grow upward out of the snout and curve backward, resting against the forehead. These are the only upward-growing top teeth known among mammals!

1

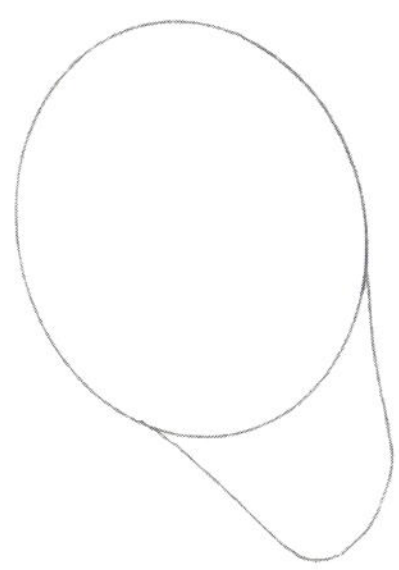

2

3

4

5

6

Serval

Did You Know?

The serval lives in thick vegetation near water, such as marshes and streams. Their habitat lies south of the Sahara Desert in Africa.

Sometimes called the "giraffe cat," the serval has a long neck, a small head, big ears, powerful legs, and a tawny, black-spotted coat.

Fun Fact!

The ears of the serval, the largest of any wildcat, are cupped with rounded edges.

1

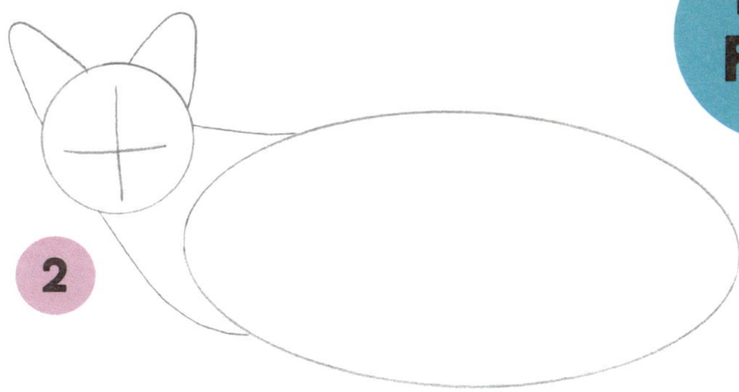

2

3

4

5

6

Monk Parakeet

Details

Size: 1 foot long
Weight: 4 ounces
Diet: Fruit, seeds, nuts, and flowers
Location: South America

Did You Know?

Also known as a "quaker parrot," the monk parakeet is a member of the parrot family. However, unlike their relatives, they build their tree nests out of sticks and twigs. All other parrots make their homes in tree cavities (or holes).

Native to South America, this playful and "talkative" bird has bright green feathers, a gray head and chest, a yellow underside, and a small orange beak.

Fun Fact!

Over the years, monk parakeets have escaped from captivity and formed wild colonies in some cities of North America and Europe.

Red-Whiskered Bulbul

Did You Know?

Outside of their native India, escaped bulbuls have formed a few wild populations in tropical areas of Australia and the United States, including one in Hawaii and one in Florida.

This tropical bird has a white chest, a white-tipped tail, and a black, pointed head crest. It is known for its red cheek markings and thin, black facial lines.

Mini Quiz

In what does the red-whiskered bulbul typically build its nest?

A. A bush

B. A tree

C. A man-made structure

D. The ground

(Answer on page 64)

Nicobar Pigeon

Details

Size: Up to 16 inches long
Weight: 1 pound
Diet: Seeds, fruit, and insects
Location: Southeast Asia

Mini Quiz

The Nicobar pigeon is found everywhere below EXCEPT:

A. Malaysia
B. Australia
C. India
D. Indonesia

(Answer on page 64)

This forest dweller has metallic feathers that range in color from blue and green to red and yellow. Its distinctly long neck feathers create the appearance of a mane.

Fun Fact!

Have you ever heard of the legendary Dodo bird? This now-extinct flightless bird was last seen in the 1600s. Using a preserved tissue sample, scientists have determined that its closest living relative on earth is the Nicobar pigeon!

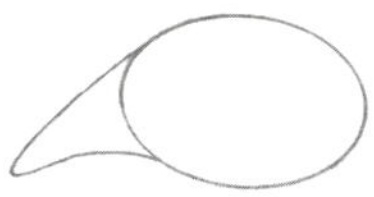

1

2

3

4

5

6

Golden Pheasant

Details

Size: 3 feet long
Weight: 3 pounds
Diet: Grains, leaves, and small animals
Location: China

Did You Know?

This pheasant's extremely long tail feathers measure more than half of the bird's total length!

The golden pheasant is originally from western China. Males are brightly colored with striped and spotted tail feathers and a head crest of golden feathers.

1

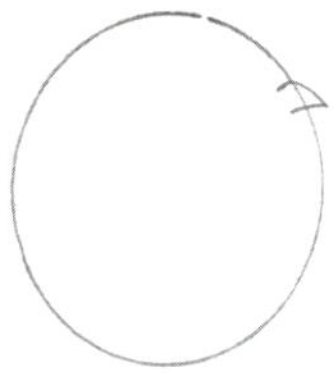

2

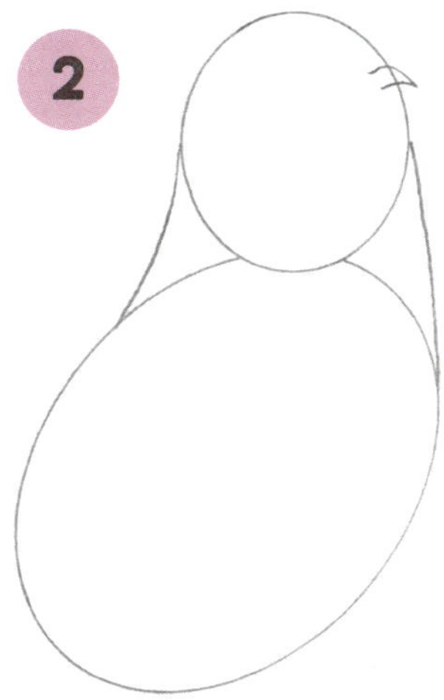

3

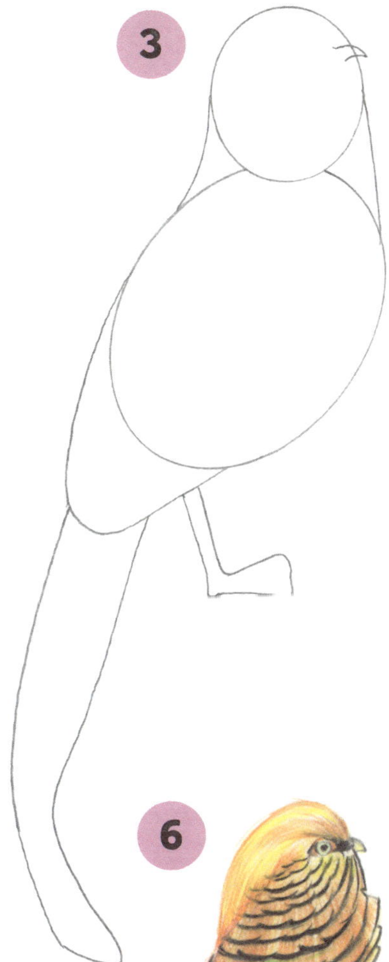

4

5

6

Fun Fact!

Pheasants are primarily terrestrial birds, meaning they spend most of their time on the ground.

Gavial

Details

Size: 15 feet long
Weight: 2,000 pounds
Diet: Fish
Location: India and Nepal

Mini Quiz

True or False:
The gavial is swift and agile on land.

(Answer on page 64)

This crocodile of the Ganges River is also called the "gharial." It has a long, narrow snout with a bulbous end and more than a hundred sharp teeth.

1

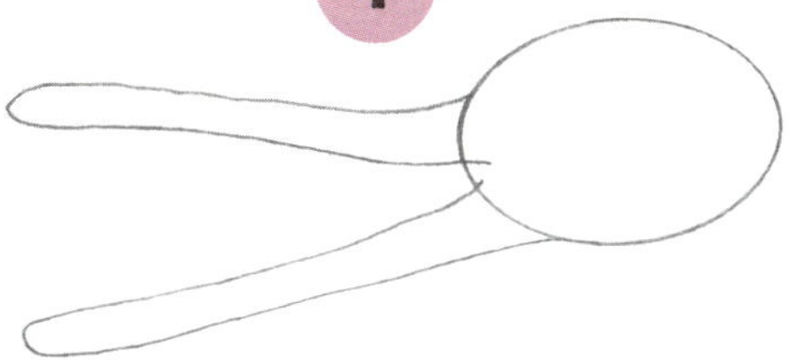

2

3

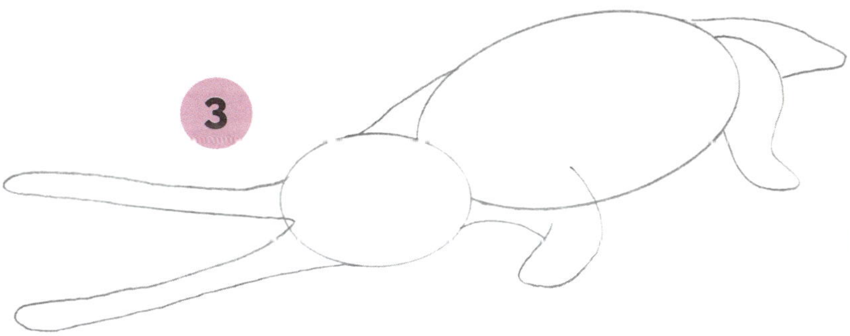

Did You Know?

To hunt for fish, the gavial sweeps its snout back and forth as it moves through the water. This excellent swimmer has a flat tail and webbed rear feet.

4

5

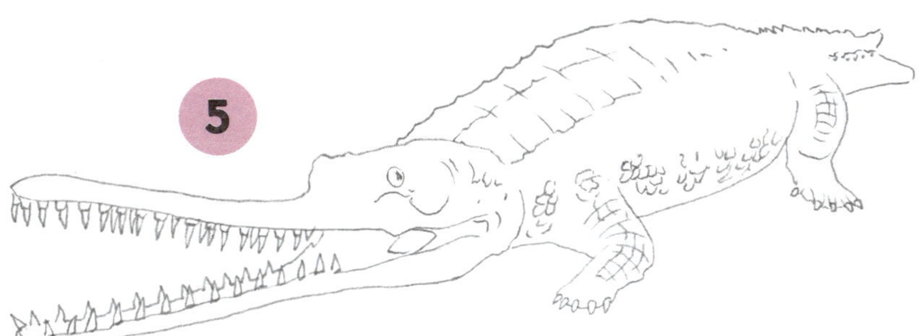

6

Giant Toad

Details

Size: 5 inches long
Weight: 4 pounds
Diet: Small animals, such as frogs, lizards, birds, and insects
Location: Central and South America

Did You Know?

This poisonous toad has been used as a form of failed pest control. Released into foreign habitats to kill beetles in Australia, the toads moved away from their site of introduction and are now considered an *invasive species.*

Resembling a rock, this large toad is brown, gray, and covered in warts. It has a gland behind each ear that secretes a poisonous substance, making its skin toxic.

1

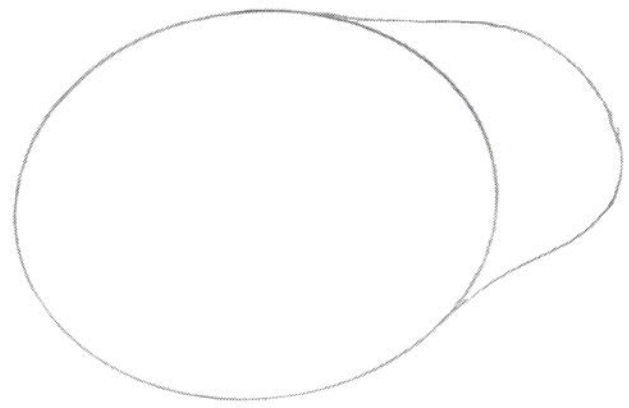

2

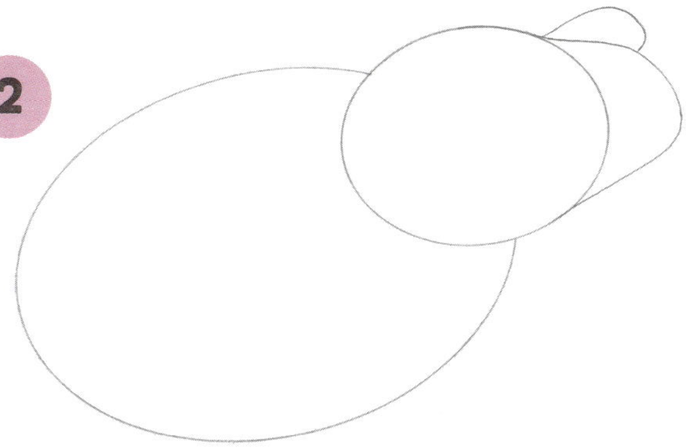

3

4

5

6

Mini Quiz

True or False: Male giant toads are much larger than female giant toads.

(Answer on page 64)

Kinkajou

Details

Size: 20 inches long
Weight: 6 pounds
Diet: Fruit, honey, nectar, insects, and eggs
Location: Central and South America

Did You Know!

These nocturnal creatures live in the trees of the rainforest. They aren't seen by humans often, but they can be heard screeching and grunting through the night!

A relative of the raccoon, the adorable kinkajou has sharp claws, round eyes, a long tongue, and a prehensile (or grasping) tail.

1

2

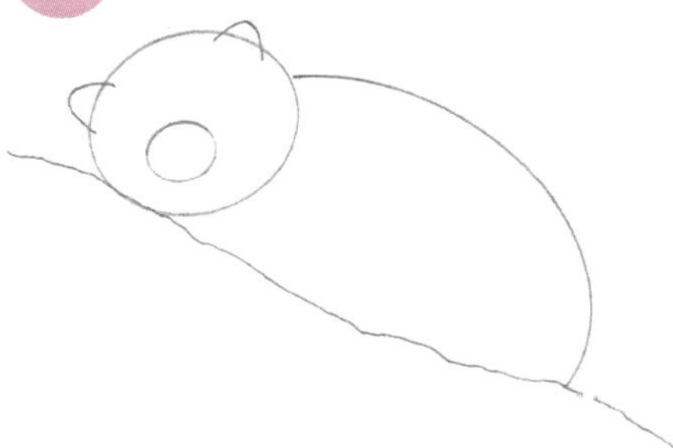

3

Fun Fact!

Kinkajou babies are born with their eyelids shut—and they stay shut for a whole month!

4

5

6

Fennec Fox

Details

Size: 15 inches long
Weight: 3 pounds
Diet: Small animals, insects, and fruit
Location: Africa and the Middle East

Fun Fact!

The fennec's tail is about a foot long—almost as long as its body!

This fox has a small head, large ears, and a bushy, black-tipped tail. It lives in the deserts of North Africa and the Middle East.

1

2

3

4

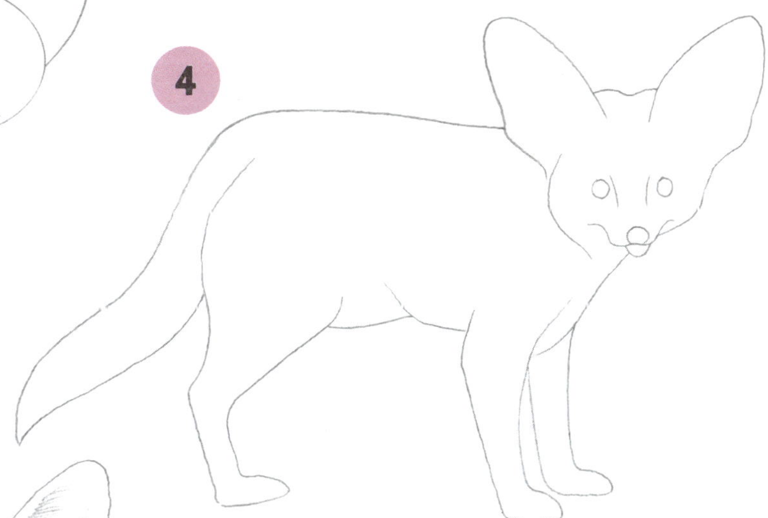

5

6

Mini Quiz

The fennec lives in what type of home?

A. Nest
B. Tree hollow
C. Cave
D. Burrow

(Answer on page 64)

Southern Tamandua

Did You Know?

Making it a great climber, the southern tamandua has long toes, sharp claws, and a prehensile (or grasping) tail. When it feels threatened, it can stand on its hind legs and swipe its paws in defense.

This toothless animal has a furry body, strong forelegs, rounded ears, and a long, slender snout and lives in the wilderness of South America.

Fun Fact!

The tamandua's sticky tongue can extend more than 15 inches!

Mini Quiz Answers

Page 11: True. From black and white to red and yellow and from circles to stripes, boa constrictors feature a range of colors and markings.

Page 13: False. The squirrel monkey is diurnal, so it is most active during the day.

Page 14: B. Woolly monkeys live in troops.

Page 19: D. All of the above.

Page 25: A. Gaurs typically have blue eyes.

Page 30: D. Hyacinth macaws can generally live to be 50 years old.

Page 41: C. Vicuñas are not related to deer.

Page 49: A. The red-whiskered bulbul builds its nest in a bush.

Page 50: B. Australia.

Page 54: False. The gavial is an excellent swimmer, but it is not quick on dry ground.

Page 57: False. Like many amphibians, the female giant toad is larger than the male.

Page 61: D. Fennecs live in burrows in the ground.